© Forever
Thankful

THIS NOTEBOOK

belongs to

_____

Date: _____

Date: _____

Date: _____

Date: _____

Date: _____

Date: _____

Date: _____

Date: _____

Date: _____

Date: _____

Date: _____

Date: _____

Date: _____

Date: _____

Date: _____

Date: _____

Date: _____

Date: _____

Date: _____

Date: _____

Date: _____

Date: _____

Date: _____

Date: _____

Date: _____

Date: _____

Date: _____

Date: _____

Date: _____

Date: _____

Date: _____

Date: _____

Date: _____

Date: _____

Date: _____

Date: _____

Date: _____

Date: _____

Date: _____

Date: _____

Date: _____

Date: _____

Date: _____

Date: _____

Date: _____

Date: _____

Date: _____

Date: _____

Date: _____

Date: _____

_____

_____

_____

_____

_____

_____

_____

_____

_____

_____

_____

_____

_____

_____

_____

_____

Date: _____

Date: _____

Date: _____

Date: _____

Date: _____

Date: _____

Date: _____

Date: _____

Date: _____

Date: _____

Date: _____

Date: _____

Date: _____

Date: _____

Date: _____

Date: _____

Date: _____

Date: _____

Date: _____

Date: _____

Date: _____

Date: _____

Date: _____

Date: _____

Date: _____

Date: _____

Date: _____

Date: _____

Date: _____

Date: _____

Date: _____

Date: _____

Date: _____

Date: _____

Date: _____

Date: _____

Date: _____

Date: _____

Date: _____

Date: _____

Date: _____

Date: _____

_____

_____

_____

_____

_____

_____

_____

_____

_____

_____

_____

_____

_____

_____

_____

_____

Date: _____

Date: _____

Date: _____

Date: _____

Date: _____

Date: _____

Date: _____

Date: _____

Date: _____

Date: _____

Date: _____

Date: _____

Date: _____

Date: _____

Date: _____

Date: _____

Date: _____

Date: _____

Date: _____

Date: _____

Date: _____

Date: _____

Date: _____

Printed in Great Britain
by Amazon

66936908R00071